Kindergarten
Hooked on Learning®
Handwriting

D1709432

Designed and illustrated by
Big Yellow Taxi, Inc.

Lines

Trace, then draw the lines.

Trace, then draw the lines.

Diagonal Lines

Trace, then draw the lines.

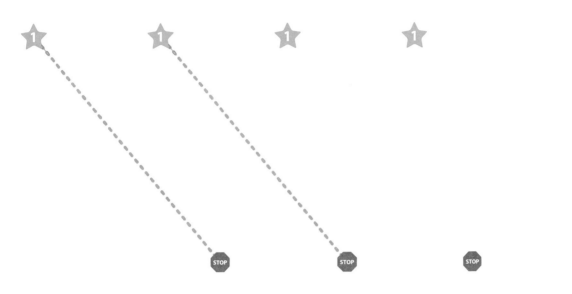

Trace, then draw the lines.

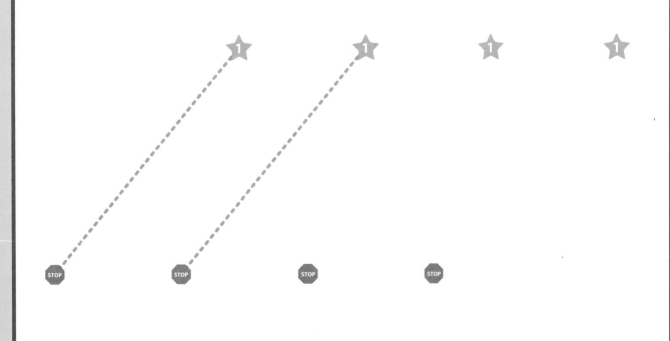

Hooked on Learning *Handwriting*

Curves

Trace, then draw the curves.

Circles

Trace, then draw the circles.

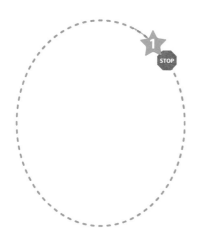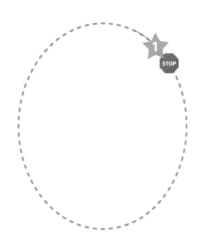

Follow the Lines

Trace the path to get Hip-O to the zoo.

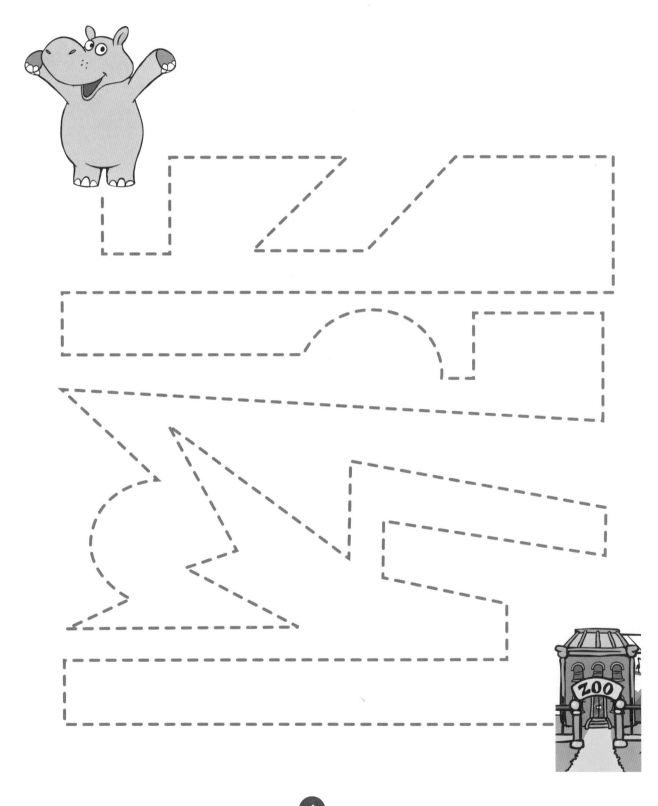

Trace the path to get Pig Wig to the
baseball game.

Hooked on Learning *Handwriting*

T and I

Trace, then write the letter "T."

Trace, then write the letter "I."

Hooked on Learning *Handwriting*

A Note to Hip-O

Trace the letters "T" and "I" to help Pig Wig complete her note.

To Hip-O,
I want to go to
the park. Try to
meet me.
It will be fun.
From Pig Wig

Hooked on Learning *Handwriting*

F and E

Trace, then write the letter "F."

Trace, then write the letter "E."

Hooked on Learning *Handwriting*

Gift Wrap

Trace the letters "F" and "E" to complete the gift tags.

For Emma

For Ed

For Eli

For Ellen

11

L and H

Trace, then write the letter "L."

Trace, then write the letter "H."

Hooked on Learning *Handwriting*

To the Zoo!

Trace the letters "L" and "H" to complete the zoo signs.

LION

HORSE

HYENA

LEOPARD

Hooked on Learning *Handwriting*

Tic-tac-toe

This is a game for two players.

What you need:
Two different-colored crayons

How to play:

1. Each player chooses one of the letters from the box below.

2. The first player writes his letter in one of the game-board squares on the opposite page.

3. The next player takes a turn.

4. Keep taking turns until one player has three of his letters in a row—up, down, or diagonally.

| T | I | F | E | L | H |

Note to Parents
Tic-tac-toe is a fun way for your child to practice handwriting skills. As your child learns to write more letters, add them to your Tic-tac-toe games.

V and W

Trace, then write the letter "V."

Trace, then write the letter "W."

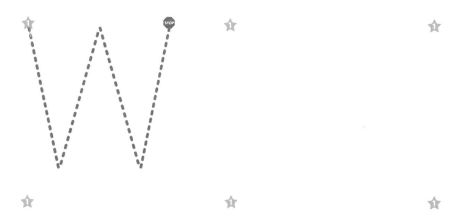

Weather Report

Trace the letters "V" and "W" to complete Pop Fox's weather report.

WEATHER
WATCH

View the
Weather Vane

W N
  E
S

X and Y

Trace, then write the letter "X."

Trace, then write the letter "Y."

Building Blocks

Trace the letters "K," "Z," and "A" to complete Hip-O's block tower.

25

On the Road

Trace the letters to complete the postcards.

We're at the Zoo!

The Kazoo and Xylophone Music Fair

Hooked on Learning Handwriting

Night on the Volcano

We Went Apple Picking Yesterday!

Hooked on Learning *Handwriting*

C and O

Trace, then write the letter "C."

Trace, then write the letter "O."

Pop Fox Shops

Trace the letters "S" and "J" to complete Pop Fox's list.

 Soup

 Jam

 Salt

 Juice

 Sunflowers

 Jellybeans

Hooked on Learning *Handwriting*

U and D

Trace, then write the letter "U."

Trace, then write the letter "D."

Book Report

Trace the letters "U" and "D" to complete the book titles.

Dance with a Unicorn

Up the Dark Stairs

35

Trace, then write the letter "P."

Trace, then write the letter "B."

Trace, then write the letter "R."

In Your Place

Make place cards for your dinner table.

Fold one index card in half for each family member.

Write the family member's name on the front half.

Then put the cards on the table to show where each person should sit.

Note to Parents
Encourage your child to practice handwriting by writing signs for your home. He might create a reminder to turn off the water while brushing teeth or a breakfast menu to post on the refrigerator.

Hooked on Learning *Handwriting*

l, t, and i

Trace, then write the letter "l."

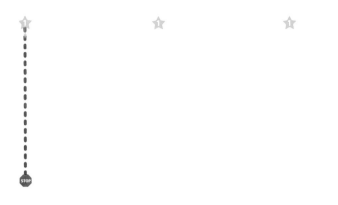

Trace, then write the letter "t."

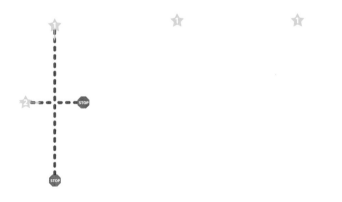

Trace, then write the letter "i."

Hooked on Learning *Handwriting*

In Our Cubbies

Trace the letters "l," "t," and "i" to complete the names on the cubbies.

Hooked on Learning *Handwriting*

j, f, and k

Trace, then write the letter "j."

Trace, then write the letter "f."

Trace, then write the letter "k."

Hooked on Learning *Handwriting*

Photo Album

Trace the letters "j," "f," and "k" to complete the captions.

I jumped rope.

I flew a kite.

I kicked a ball.

I took my jam to the fair.

Hooked on Learning *Handwriting*

v and w

Trace, then write the letter "v."

Trace, then write the letter "w."

Very Well

Trace the letter "v" to get Dog Bug to the van.
Trace the letter "w" to get Dog Bug to the wagon.

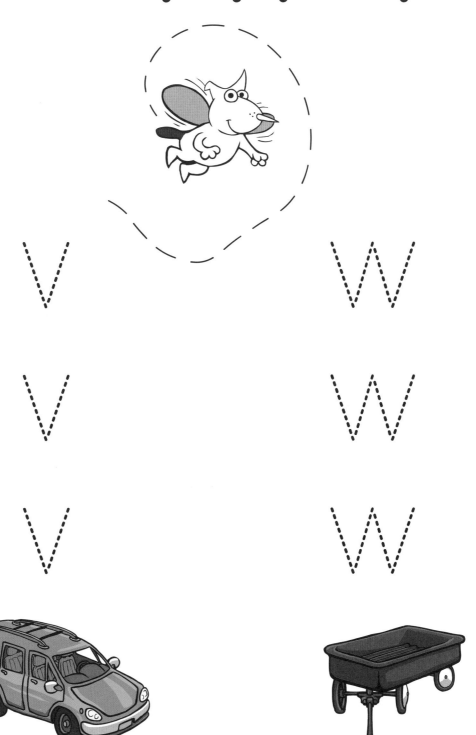

V   W

V   W

V   W

47

x, y, and z

Trace, then write the letter "x."

Trace, then write the letter "y."

Trace, then write the letter "z."

Hooked on Learning *Handwriting*

The Phone Book

Trace the letters "x," "y," and "z" to complete Pop Fox's phone book.

Alexa   555-2345

Avery   555-3589

Buzz   555-4022

Kaz   555-5256

Max   555-___

Tony   555-___86

49

Match Game

Trace the letters on the left.
Then draw lines to match the letter pairs.

v

w

x

y

z

x

z

y

v

w

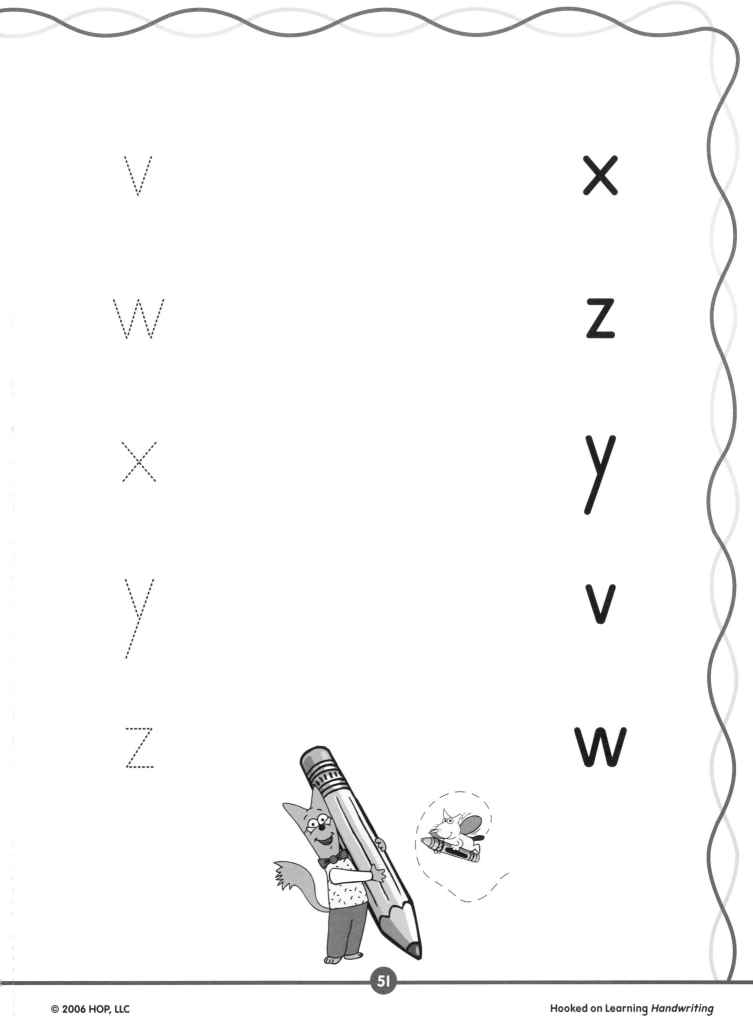

51

h, m, and n

Trace, then write the letter "h."

Trace, then write the letter "m."

Trace, then write the letter "n."

Hooked on Learning *Handwriting*

Keeping Score

Trace the letters "s," "c," "o," and "a" to complete the scoreboard.

Today's Soccer Score:

Ball Hogs   2

Gray Storm   1

57

g, d, q, and e

Trace, then write the letter "g."

Trace, then write the letter "d."

Trace, then write the letter "q."

Trace, then write the letter "e."

58

Anchors Away!

Trace the letters "g," "d," "q," and "e" to complete the names of Hip-O's and Pig Wig's boats.

Aqua Marine

The Hodge Podge

59

From A to Z!

Trace the letters in ABC order to make a path from Hip-O to his friends.

Hooked on Learning *Handwriting*